MAKE IT A
GREAT DAY

*A 40-Day Devotional Filled with
Scripture, Stories, and Strategies
to Own Your Day*

Lisa T. Ballard

Make it a Great Day: A 40-Day Devotional Filled with Scripture, Stories, and Strategies to Own Your Day
by Lisa T. Ballard

Cover design, editing, book layout, and publishing services by KishKnows, Inc., Richton Park, Illinois, 708-252-DOIT
admin@kishknows.com, www.kishknows.com

ISBN: 978-0-578-81586-2
LCCN: 2020924257

All rights reserved. No part of this book may be reproduced, distributed, or transmitted in any form or by any means, including photocopying, recording, digital scanning, or other electronic or mechanical methods, without the prior written permission of the publisher, except in the case of brief quotations embodied in critical reviews and certain other noncommercial uses permitted by copyright law. For permission requests, please contact Lisa Ballard at *lballardministries@gmail.com*.

Some Scripture references may be paraphrased versions or illustrative references of the author. Unless otherwise specified, all other references are from **King James Version of the Bible**.

The **ESV®** Bible (**The Holy Bible, English Standard Version®**). ESV® Text Edition: 2016. Copyright© 2001 by Crossway, a publishing ministry of Good News Publishers. The ESV® text has been reproduced in cooperation with and by permission of Good News Publishers. Unauthorized reproduction of this publication is prohibited. All rights reserved.

Scriptures marked **NIV** are taken from **THE HOLY BIBLE, NEW INTERNATIONAL VERSION®**, (NIV)® Copyright© 1973, 1978, 1984, 2011 by Biblica, Inc.® Used by permission. All rights reserved worldwide.

Scripture quotations marked **NLT** are taken from the *Holy Bible*, **New Living Translation**, copyright© 1996, 2004, 2015 by Tyndale House Foundation. Used by permission of Tyndale House Publishers, Inc., Carol Stream, Illinois 60188. All rights reserved.

Scriptures marked **MSG** are taken from *THE MESSAGE*, copyright© 1993, 2002, 2018 by Eugene H. Peterson. Used by permission of NavPress. All rights reserved. Represented by Tyndale House Publishers, Inc.

Copyright© 2020 by Lisa Ballard
Printed in the United States of America

Table of Contents

Foreword	iii
Introduction	iv
A Word from the Author	vi
Use His Name	1
Delightful Day	3
Right Choice, Right Connection, Right Conclusion	6
May I Be Too Big to See the Things that Others Do to Me	9
Great Peace Day!	11
Don't Get Stuck in Your Struck Place	14
Promise, Purpose, and Praise	16
Yesterday!	19
Whatever!	22
The Power of Focus	24
Shift	27
Position for Possession	30
Hold Tight, Hold Right, and Don't Lose Sight	33
When Your Plans Don't Match God's Plans	35
Keep Your Eyes on Jesus	37
Return to Sender	40
Press Past the Issue to Your Purpose	42
So, You Decided to Stay	45
I Am a Designer Original	47

Random Acts of Kindness	49
Sing a Song	51
Be Generous	53
The Benefits of Waiting on God	55
The Power of Prayer	57
Save the Babies	60
Own Your Day	62
Serve the Lord with Gladness	64
Muzzle Your Mouth	66
I Will…I Shall…I *Must* Overcome	68
Have Your Way Lord	70
The Heart of the Matter	72
Help Me to Handle this Moment	74
You Have What You Need for a Great Day!	77
I Am	79
Break the Rules	81
The Man in the Mirror	84
Live Your Best Life Today	86
Heal and Restore	88
Dear God, Accomplish Your Will in My Life	90
React or Respond	92
Burned but Not Buried	94
About the Author	97
Contact the Author	99

Foreword

"Make It a Great Day" is just what we need in times like this. Pessimism, negative thinking, fear, and anxiety pervade our every waking moment. Written with the personification and embodiment of faith, this book examines a new way of facing and dealing with those moments. Elder Lisa Ballard's wit, humor, passion, and faith in God inspires us to turn every lemon into lemonade.

As we take this great journey together, we will learn how to pray and exercise our faith, think differently, and see beyond our present reality. Sometimes, God gives us wisdom; and other times, He gives us words. With this book, God has given us both. Regardless of your station in life, after reading this book, you will be blessed with the words to gain the wisdom to truly *Make It a Great Day*.

Blessings,

Lady Jamell Meeks
Salem Baptist Church of Chicago
Chicago, IL

∘— Introduction —∘

Innumerable things can be said about the author of this book. Having been married to her for over forty years, I can attest that I have lived with a woman of great faith. She has a deep love for Christ and takes her relationship with Him very seriously.

We should all learn as we live. As I have lived with Lisa, she has taught me many things. Her unconditional love for me is the epitome of the love that Christ has for mankind. Her daily study of the Word inspires me, and her consistent prayer life encourages me.

Lisa has the best interest of the church at heart. She believes that the kingdom of Heaven is at hand and that God put the works of the kingdom in her hands. This is the reason that I believe in the anointing that is on her life, and its ability to change the lives of others.

Through Lisa's teaching and preaching burdens have been removed, and yokes have been destroyed. Her anointing gives her the ability to preach with power and authority.

I could not—and would not—ask God for any other helpmeet. I have been a pastor for thirty-four years, and Lisa could write the book on being a co-pastor. She defines the position…I am sure if you looked up co-pastor in the dictionary, you would see her picture, because there is only one Lisa Trinnette Taylor Ballard!

Lisa is a voice to the people. She inspires young and old, men and women alike with her gifts and talents. When she steps into an arena where women are not often given the same welcome as men, she neither apologizes for her femininity nor acquiesces to bitterness. Instead, she calmly seeks to serve.

"For it is God's will that by doing good you should silence the ignorant talk of foolish people."
1 Peter 2:15 (NIV)

Her humble spirit and biblical prowess have earned her respect even among those who are skeptical of women in ministry.

"Ain't but one LTTB!"

I stand in amazement at the many hats that she wears: wife, mother, grandmother, career woman, and co-pastor of Sunrise. She is exceptional in all of these areas and continues to produce a fruitful, purposeful, and meaningful life.

I believe that you will benefit from reading this book and be transformed beyond the dismal into the delightful—from the tranquil to the transformational.

To those of you who have not met her, I am delighted to be a forerunner to prepare your heart for the awesome ministry of Lisa Trinnette Taylor Ballard.

Pastor David Ballard, Sr.

○— A Word from the Author —○

I have entered *"Chapter Sixty"* of my life—and what a journey it has been! God has showered me with His incredible favor; and for that, I am grateful.

If you have ever telephoned me and gotten my voicemail, you may have noticed that I end my greeting by saying, *"Make it a great day!"*

These are trying times when we consider:

- The economic climate that we are living in.
- The COVID virus that has impacted the entire world.
- Our ability to go to a church building on a Sunday morning.
- The viral exposure of systemic racism.
- Our day-to-day personal issues.

The question becomes, *"How can I make my day great?"*

I think that it is important to start the day off right by spending time with God; praying, reading His Word, and praising and worshiping Him.

> *"Seek ye first the Kingdom of God and His righteousness and all these things will be added unto you."*
> **Matthew 6:33 (KJV)**

It is my prayer that you will include this book as a part of your daily devotions and time with God and that you will experience what I call a "Three-P-Day."

Peaceful, Productive, and Purposeful

Peaceful

"And the peace of God, which passeth all understanding, shall keep your hearts and minds through Christ Jesus."
Philippians 4:7 (KJV)

Productive

"Go to the ant, o sluggard. Consider her ways and be wise. Without having any chief, officer, or ruler, she prepares her bread in summer and gathers her food in harvest."
Proverbs 6:6-8 (ESV)

Purposeful

"But I have raised you up for this very purpose, that I might show you my power and that my name be proclaimed in all the earth."
Exodus 9:16 (NIV)

May God deal bountifully with each of you and all those who are attached to you, that you may live and keep His Word!

Make it a great day!

○— **Dedication** —○

I dedicate this book to my pastor and husband, David Ballard, Sr. Forty-one years ago, we started out so young into the uncharted territory of marriage. God has blessed us to walk through the good, the bad, and the ugly. I thank God that He kept us, and I am grateful for your direction, criticism, covering…and most importantly, your love! Husband, you are a mighty man!

Always and forever,
Lisa Trinnette Taylor Ballard

⸻ Special Dedication ⸻

To my father, Deacon Frank Taylor,

Daddy, we didn't have a lot of time together...but the quality would measure one hundred years. Death cannot kill who you were to me, and the grave cannot take away the memories of you that are in my heart.

Love Mona...Your Pumpkin Nanny.
— Lisa Trinnette

⟞ Use His Name ⟝

"The name of the Lord is a strong tower; the righteous runneth into it and is safe."
Proverbs 18:10 (KJV)

A few years ago, I traveled to minister at a women's conference in Cincinnati, Ohio with my daughters and a few of the ladies from our church. I flew instead of driving, so I arrived before they did. When they got to the hotel, I was not in the room (I was at the mall :-)), and Denesha (my oldest daughter) asked the front desk attendant if she could have a key to her mom's room. The attendant would not give it to her because her name was not on the reservation. D'Lisa (my second daughter) decided to use her name to her advantage. She asked for a key to her (my) room…and the clerk gave it to her, because she used the "right name!"

Those who have accepted Jesus as their personal Savior are considered righteous. You were made *righteous* because you chose the *right way*. One of the many advantages of being righteous is that you have the *name of Jesus* at your disposal! You can gain access to places that money can't buy and position can't acquire.

What good is it to have the name of Jesus and not use it? *"The name of the Lord is a fortified tower, the righteous run to it and are safe."* Your safety and security are in the name of the Lord! Today, I encourage you to use the name of Jesus in every situation of your life because you will gain access to His *peace*, His *security*, and His *safety*. At the name of Jesus, every knee—the seen and the unseen—must bow. There is *power* in the name of Jesus; use it today! He *always* makes things better.

Make it a great day!

How Can I Use the Name of Jesus Today?

○— Delightful Day —○

"I delight to do thy will, O my God:
yea, thy law is within my heart."
Psalm 40:8 (KJV)

"Delight thyself also in the Lord,
and he will give you the desires of your heart."
Psalm 37:4 (KJV)

What is your delight? What is it that gives you pleasure? Today, let us delight in knowing the will of God.

Don't make your move too soon.
B.B. King wrote a song called, *"Never Make Your Move Too Soon."* How many of us can admit that we have made a move too soon? We do something too quickly, then have an "aha moment" and think, *"I should have waited."*

When I find myself in a bad place, I have to rewind and ask myself three questions:

- Did I ask God before I made this move?
- Did I ask Him if this was His will for my life?
- Did I wait for an answer?

"The safest place to be is inside the will of God." I can hear my friend Deborah Brooks Beals (RIP, dear friend!), singing this with the choir of the King of Glory.

The will of God is the place where He wants you to be, all the time! But how do you *know* His will?

I submit to you that if you allow God to put His will in your heart and delight in His way, He will give you the desires of your heart, according to His Word.

Practice chasing after the will of God. Ask Him to show you. *"Lord, show me the way that you want me to go, and the things that you want me to accomplish. In Jesus' name. Amen."* After you ask Him… watch what happens!

Don't just have the *name* of God and not His *nature*. Delight in knowing both His will *and* His nature, and He *will* give you the desires of your heart!

Make it a great day!

What Can I Do to Make Today a Delightful Day?

Right Choice, Right Connection, ○— Right Conclusion —○

*"I am the vine; you are the branches.
If you remain in me and I in you, you will bear much fruit;
apart from me you can do nothing."*
John 15:5 (NIV)

Most of us use multiple electronic devices these days, and that means we have more than one charger.

I have a charger for my Android (*Yes, I use an Android!*), a charger for my "fruit" phone, and one for my iPad. One sleepy night, I tried to put the right cord in the wrong device. The cord didn't fit because the Android cord wasn't designed for the Apple device!

I tried several times until it hit me that this wasn't the right device. The lesson here is that we should not try to make something work if it was not designed for our purpose.

"And the king of Egypt spake to the Hebrew midwives, of which the name of the one was Shiphrah, and the name of the other Puah: And he said, 'When ye do the office of a midwife to the Hebrew women, and see them upon the stools; if it be a son, then ye shall kill him: but if it be a daughter, then she shall live.' But the midwives feared God, and did not as the king of Egypt commanded them, but saved the men children alive. And the king of Egypt called for the midwives, and said unto them, 'Why have ye done this thing, and have saved the men children alive?' And the midwives said unto Pharaoh, 'Because the Hebrew women are not as the Egyptian women; for they are lively, and are delivered ere the midwives come in unto them.' Therefore, God dealt well with the midwives: and the people multiplied, and waxed very mighty.

And it came to pass, because the midwives feared God, that he made them houses."
Exodus 1:15-21 (KJV)

Shiprah and Puah were midwives in Egypt who were assigned by Pharaoh to kill all of the boy babies born to the Hebrew women in order to keep the Hebrews from multiplying.

They made the decision to follow God instead of listening to Pharaoh, and to let the boys live. They had the right *connection* because they joined together and made the right *choice,* and the *conclusion* was that not only did the people of God continue to multiply, but He dealt well with the midwives, and they received His favor.

Right *choice:* Who do you have on your personal "board of directors" (those closest to you)?

Right *connection:* Are you connected to the right things that will help you excel?

The right *choice*…the connection…will bring you the right *conclusion*…the good fruit.

Make it a great day!

The Right Choices…

....

....

....

....

....

And the Right Connections…

....

....

....

....

....

Bring the Right Conclusions!

....

....

....

....

....

....

....

May I Be Too Big to See the Things that ○— Others Do to Me —○

My grandfather, Elder Allen Jefferson, wrote this poem many years ago:

Lord, may I live to help the man
Who tries to keep me down.
May I greet him with a smile,
Who greets me with a frown.
May I be too big to see,
The things that others do to me.

May I never hold a grudge,
Nor hunt for scattered strife.
May I never seek to judge,
The faults in other's lives.
May I be too big to see,
The things that others do to me.

Granddaddy was trying to teach me, over fifty years later, *"Lisalotcy (his nickname for me), not everyone is going to love you and support you. You may come across individuals who just don't like you and say all manner of evil against you. But when they go **low**...you go **high**."*

Make it a great day!

I'm Too Big for This!

○— Great Peace Day! —○

*"Great peace have they who love your law,
and nothing can make you stumble."*
Psalm 119:165 (NIV)

It is my firm belief that attitudes don't just happen—you choose them.

The Psalmist tells us that there is *peace,* and then there is *great peace.*

Peace is when all the bills are paid, everyone around you is doing what they should be doing, your body feels well, and you haven't gotten a low balance notice on your phone. That's *peaceful.*

Great peace, I would argue, is when you get the low balance alert with payments pending, or you are summoned to your child's school yet again, or you are expected to handle a situation that is "way above your pay grade," and yet you still have peace.

Great peace requires two things of you: *to release* the anxiety, and replace it with the Word.

*"Be anxious for nothing, but in everything by prayer and
supplication, with thanksgiving, let your requests
be made known to God."*
Philippians 4:6 (NIV)

Release the spirit of defeat and *replace* it with: *"Thanks be unto God, who gives me the victory."*

Even in your single hours, *release* the loneliness, and *replace* it with *"The Lord is with me."*

Identify the things that are after your peace; *release* them from your thoughts and your speech, and *replace* them with good words that come from the Word of God.

*"God is not human, that he should lie,
not a human being,
that he should change his mind.
Does he speak and then not act?
Does he promise and not fulfill?"*
Numbers 23:19 (NLT)

If God *said* it, He will *do* it!

Make it a great day!

What Do I Need to Release Today...and What Can I Replace it With?

⊸ Don't Get Stuck in Your Struck Place ⊷

"Brethren, I count not myself to have apprehended but this one thing I do, forgetting those things which are behind and reaching forth unto these things which are before. I press toward the mark for the prize of the high calling of God in Christ Jesus."
Philippians 3:13-14 (KJV)

Life, I've discovered, is not a playground, but a battleground. Some of these battles have struck us hard…but you can't get *stuck* in your *struck place*.

You are in your *struck place* when the strikes bring you to a place of discontentment, and all of those issues keep you from getting to the place that God has set for you…but *you have the power to move forward!*

Whether the challenge is writing a book, doing ministry work, ending a relationship, changing jobs, experiencing health issues, having to adjust to the loss of someone close to you, or financial challenges, the mantra for today is *move forward*. You have that power.

"God, having provided some better thing for us…"
Hebrews 11:40a (KJV)

Light the fire and move forward; you can't get *"stuck in your struck place"* because your *"right now"* can't handle your *"bigger."*

Make it a great day!

Where Am I Stuck Today?

◦— **Promise, Purpose, and Praise** —◦

"And Moses said unto the people, 'Fear ye not, stand still, and see the salvation of the Lord, which he will shew to you today: for the Egyptians whom ye have seen today, ye shall see them again no more forever. The Lord shall fight for you, and ye shall hold your peace.'"
Exodus 14:13-14 (KJV)

Have you ever woken up with plans and a list of things that you wanted to accomplish that day and then a problem arises that throws you off course? I hate that! *(My name is Lisa Ballard…and I need to be more flexible!)*

I believe that for every *problem,* there is a *promise*; for every *promise,* there is a *purpose*; for every *purpose,* there is a *praise*.

The Hebrews were faced with a situation after coming out of Egypt. They thought they were free; and yet, their enemy came after them. Suddenly, they were in the wilderness—with the Red Sea in front of them, the Egyptian army behind them, and the mountains surrounding them.

They blamed their deliverer, saying, *"Were there no graves in Egypt? You had to bring us out here to die?"* **(Exodus 14:11 paraphrased)**

That was a *problem!* But for every problem, there is a *promise.*

First, Moses told them not to be scared. *(Today, take authority of those things that are making you anxious!)* Then, he told them to stand still so that they would see the salvation of the Lord that He would show them that day. *(Don't panic; just watch God work.)* He promised them that they would never see the Egyptians who were pursuing them again. That's *deliverance!*

When you have deliverance, one of two things is going to happen: either God is going to remove that thing completely and you will never have to face it again…or the problem may remain—but how you handle it will be different!

For every *problem,* there is a *purpose.*

The purpose here is that you will see God work, and you can share the story of how He delivered you with someone else. The purpose here is that you need to hold your peace, and let the Lord fight the battle!

What a great witnessing tool! For every *problem,* there is a *praise.*

Later on in the chapter, Miriam got the women together, and they praised God, singing, *"The Lord God Almighty brought us out!"*

Go out today with this thought in your mind…

- For every *problem,* there is a *purpose.*
- For every *purpose,* there is a *promise.*
- For every *promise,* there is a *praise.*

Make it a great day!

What is My Problem...Purpose...Praise for Today?

○— **Yesterday!** —○

*"Brethren, I count not myself to have apprehended:
but this one thing I do, forgetting those things which are behind,
and reaching forth unto those things which are before..."*
Philippians 3:13 (KJV)

There is a song by *Boyz II Men* called *It's So Hard to Say Goodbye to Yesterday*. Although the song came out almost thirty years ago, it is still sung at many funerals and memorials today.

Many of us have a difficult time saying goodbye to yesterday— whether it was the yesterday where you needed your father and someone or something took your place, or the yesterday when things were good and then something came along and shattered your world.

For some of us, our yesterday is holding us hostage in the present and keeping us from our future. The apostle Paul tells us in **Philippians 3** to *"Move forward, and let go of yesterday"* (paraphrased). Learn from it, *laugh* about it, and then *leave* it!

My oldest daughter (affectionately known in our family as *"That Denesha"*) said to me, *"I don't want to be an adult anymore. It was so much easier when I lived at home."* It was one of those days where she wanted to sleep, but she had bills to pay and a business to run, so she had to go to work.

I said to her, *"Denesha, that was yesterday! All you can do is learn from it, and laugh about all of the things we did as a family, then leave it in the past."*

....
Recorded Fall 1990; Single, released August 1991.
Boyz II Men: "Its's So Hard To Say Goodbye To Yesterday,"

Dear God in heaven, it is our prayer today that you will release us from the burdens of yesterday. Help us to learn from them and move forward. In Jesus' Name, I pray. Amen.

Make it a great day!

What Do I Need to Leave in Yesterday?

○— **Whatever!** —○

*"Therefore I tell you, **whatever** you ask for in prayer, believe that you have received it, and it will be yours."*
Mark 11:24 (NIV)

Have you ever been part of a conversation that is headed in the wrong direction and someone says, *"Whatever!"*?

That "whatever" is meant to either dismiss a previous statement or to say, *"I don't care!"*

When Jesus said, *"Whatever"* in **Mark 11:24**, He was telling us, *"I care about you, and I will not dismiss you."* You have a "whatever" clause given to you by your Heavenly Father.

Jesus said that whatever we desire, we should ask for in prayer, meaning that our desires should be coupled with prayer. He said that if we believe that we have received it, it will be ours.

Today, I encourage you to have an open dialogue with God about your desires, believing in the Word of God that He will, and you shall have it.

Use your "whatever" clause…it *will* work for you!

Make it a great day!

What is My "Whatever" for God Today?

The Power of Focus

"Finally, brethren, whatsoever things are true, whatsoever things are honest, whatsoever things are just, whatsoever things are pure, whatsoever things are lovely, whatsoever things are of good report; if there be any virtue and if there by any praise, think on these things."
Philippians 4:8 (KJV)

Focus means *"to adapt to the prevailing light so that you can see clearly."*

Things happen that are out of your control, but you are forced to deal with them. Maybe you have been patiently waiting on God for a new job opportunity, a mate, a better relationship, or more money, and you feel like God is taking His time answering you. And sometimes, the answer you get is not what you expected.

"Wait on the Lord; be of good courage and he shall strengthen thine heart."
Psalm 27:14 (KJV)

I believe that God is telling you to manifest His work in your life while you are waiting on Him to answer your prayers; and knowing that however He chooses to answer you, He will give you the strength that you need to get through the moment.

While the enemy is after your faith in God, you must remain focused. Maybe you have lost your job; focus on the gain and not on the loss. Look at the prevailing light—He made sure that all of your needs have been met in this season.

The thought for today is *"Focus on the bright side in all things; realize that God is your Source, and you will be able to clearly see the will of God in your life."*

Dear Heavenly Father, we ask that you help us to focus on those things that are right, honest, fair, and of good report, so that we may see you clearly. In Jesus' Name we pray. Amen.

Make it a great day!

What is My Focus for Today?

○— **Shift** —○

"Then she saddled an ass and said to her servant, 'Drive and go forward. Slack not thy riding for me, except I bid thee.'"
2 Kings 4:24 (KJV)

When we were starting out in ministry and our family was young and growing, we only had one car. Someone blessed us with a car during that time. We have always been givers, regardless of our income, and God has always blessed us abundantly.

The only issue was that the car was a stick shift; and unlike my husband, I had never driven a stick. I would have to learn how to drive the car so that we could utilize the gift.

Shout out to my Terri, my sister-in-love, who taught me how to drive that car. I remember being on 79th Street in Chicago with all of my babies in the car. It was very busy, and Terri said, *"You will either learn to drive this stick, or we are all going to die."* Needless to say, I learned to drive that car very quickly!

Driving a stick shift takes a great deal of coordination. Left hand for the steering wheel, right hand for the gear shift, left foot for the clutch, and right foot for the gas and the brake. It was a lot, but nothing that couldn't be accomplished.

The power was in the shift. The car can only operate for so long in the same gear before you have to shift. If you don't shift when you are supposed to, the engine will scream at you and possibly cut off, keeping you from reaching your destination.

Utilize the gift of the Holy Spirit that the Lord has given you—and recognize when He tells you to *shift!*

When things are not going the way that you want them to, and you cannot stop—*shift!*

There was a Shunammite woman whose only child became ill and died. She saddled her donkey and told her servant to go, and not to stop unless she told him to. She needed her son healed, and she could not wallow in the fact that he was dead. In fact, she declared to all who asked: *"It shall be well."*

She commanded him to *"Drive, go forth, and slack not."* In other words…*shift!*

Shift…

- For your deliverance and breakthrough!
- To take you to a greater place!
- Because those attached to you will not stop; they are watching your progress.

The word for the day is *shift!* Whatever comes your way today, *shift!*

Make it a great day!

Where or How Do I Need to Shift Today?

Position for Possession

"Have not I commanded thee? Be strong and of a good courage; be not afraid, neither be thou dismayed: for the Lord thy God is with thee whithersoever thou goest."
Joshua 1:9 (KJV)

The children of Israel were moving out of their bondage into The Promised Land. They had been waiting for this for a long time and suffered many afflictions, but I am sure that they were anxious about being in a new land—even if it *was* "overflowing with milk and honey."

Joshua, their leader, told them that they must *be prepared to possess*. Just like the Israelites, we have things that we want from God—things that have been promised to us.

- Abundant life
- The head and not the tail
- To be lenders and not borrowers
- Companionship
- New jobs
- New homes

Whatever it is that you are asking of the Lord, you must position yourself to receive His blessings that will make you rich and add no sorrows. You must do as Joshua said, and *"Be strong and of good courage." **(Joshua 1:9 KJV)***

Possessing your blessings is not a "microwave" process. You may have to wait. You may be frustrated. But whatever comes, you must stay committed.

The second part of the recipe is, *"Be not afraid nor dismayed."* This speaks of control. Positioning requires response (led by intellect), not reaction (led by emotion.)

"For the Lord your God is with you…" speaks of consistency. He went on to tell them in **Verse 11**, *"The Lord your God will give it to you to possess."*

- Pass through the host (be *consistent*).
- Prepare your victuals (be *committed*).
- Within three days you shall pass over the Jordan (be in *control*).

You must keep your emotions in check, regardless of the wait. Whatever your Jordan looks like today, you *will* pass over.

Make it a great day!

How Will I Position Myself to Possess Today?

Hold Tight, Hold Right, and
○— Don't Lose Sight! —○

*"For the which cause I also suffer these things: nevertheless,
I am not ashamed: for I know whom I have believed,
and am persuaded that he is able to keep that which
I have committed unto him against that day."*
2 Timothy 1:12 (KJV)

As I write this, we are in the middle of a global pandemic due to the Coronavirus disease, also known as COVID-19. Quarantining and social distancing have become the "new normal," and it is not something that any of us have experienced before in our lifetime.

When this first began, we rushed to the grocery store to make sure that we had everything we thought we might need. You can imagine the look on my face when I couldn't find a loaf of bread, a chicken wing, or hamburger meat in the store!

After three trips to the store in three days, I had to say, *"Wait, Lisa Ballard. Hold **tight**, hold **right**, and don't lose **sight**."*

I made sure that my house was filled with everyone's favorite goodies, just in case we ended up being the "safe haven" for our family.

Whatever the situation that you are facing…*hold tight*. It hasn't taken God by surprise that you are in this place.

Hold right. Give it to God. This is not bigger than God, and He can handle it. When you *hold right,* you are saying, *"I commit this to God. I trust that He is in control, and He will make it all right."*

Hold sight. Believe that God is going to keep you in everything. Hold sight on what He can do, and not why it is happening. He is able to keep you in everything, no matter what the day may bring.

Make it a great day!

What is My "Hold Tight, Hold Right, Don't Lose Sight" Situation Today?

....
....
....
....
....
....
....
....
....
....
....
....
....
....
....
....
....
....
....
....

When Your Plans Don't Match
⸺ God's Plans ⸺

*"In all thy ways acknowledge him,
and he shall direct thy paths."*
Proverbs 3:6 (KJV)

I am one of those people who keeps a "To-Do" list. Crossing off what I have accomplished that day gives me a sense of victory and tells me that I have had a productive day!

Some days, I don't get everything done because of external interruptions. I used to get frustrated, until I realized that it was just not meant to be for that day.

I acknowledged God in the beginning of my day, so I had to bow to His will. After all—I *had* asked Him for direction!

When you have finished this day and you didn't get to do everything that you wanted to do, confess that it's been a good day because you did the things that God had planned for you. Rejoice that He is in your life and that He had a plan to make you stronger, wiser, and better.

Plan your days…but leave room for *God's* plans because He knows what lies ahead.

Make it a great day!

What Do I Need to Accomplish Today?

○— Keep Your Eyes on Jesus —○

"Lord, if it's you," Peter replied,
"tell me to come to you on the water."
Matthew 14:28 (NIV)

"Come," He said.

Focus means *"to adapt to the prevailing light, so you can see clearly."* Today, I encourage you to stay focused. This life has many difficulties, and the outcome is tied to our focus.

We must learn to change our focus so that we can see God clearly in all things.

*"And we know that all things work together
for our good to them that love God and
who are called according to his purpose."*
Romans 8:28 (NIV)

There was a couple who recently lost everything due to unemployment. The husband felt defeated, like he had let his family down. They had to downsize, moving from their dream home to an apartment.

This husband got another job; and after a few months, he realized that he was spending more time with his family and putting more money into his savings account. Even though the apartment was smaller than the house, they were able to do more as a family.

He soon began to thank God that he didn't have to mow grass or shovel snow, and he also realized that if something broke, someone else was responsible for making the repairs. When his focus changed, he stopped sinking in self-pity and defeat.

When Peter saw Jesus, he walked toward Him on the water—something that, by nature, couldn't be done. When he took his eyes off of Jesus and concentrated on what he was doing, he began to sink.

You need to stop watching yourself, and start watching God work through you! Does your focus on your career, your ministry, or your relationship need to be realigned? Change your focus...*it will keep you from sinking.*

Make it a great day!

My Eyes Are on Jesus

Today, I will fix my eyes and thoughts on charting my day under submission to the will of God.

○— **Return to Sender** —○

*"I will give them a heart to know me, that I am the Lord.
They will be my people, and I will be their God,
for they will return to me with all their heart."*
Jeremiah 24:7 (KJV)

My family could have passed for the Brady Bunch, with our three girls and three boys. You can imagine how much it took for our parents to raise this family!

The Taylor family was known on our block for church and discipline. I can remember saying to my mother, *"But Sandra's mother is letting her go!"* and my mother would say, *"I'm not Sandra's mother, and don't bring her house into my house."* In other words, *"What goes on in that house will not fly in this house!"*

I am afraid that our spiritual houses have been infiltrated by foreign agents. Have we compromised our holiness (not a denomination, but a requirement) so that we can be socially acceptable?

Just because it is *good to us,* it is not necessarily *God for us.* Have we decided to use the excuse that *"God knows my heart?"*

Our Father is God, and He is holy. We are His children, and we should represent His holiness. Practice walking in holiness today. It's not about your outward dress; it's about the change that is on the inside, which will be reflected on the outside.

No matter how you speak, what you do, or how you do it, *let it be holy.*

Make it a great day!

How Can I Practice Walking in Holiness Today?

Press Past the Issue to
○— Your Purpose —○

"And he said unto her, 'Daughter, thy faith hath made thee whole; go in peace, and be whole of thy plague.'"
Mark 5:34 (KJV)

Issue: *an unsettled matter or dispute.*

I wish that I could tell you that today will be a perfect day, but the truth of the matter is that you may be faced with issues.

Your affirmation for today is: *"Press past your issue."*

Let's look at the woman with the issue of blood. I have always thought of her as one of the "unsung heroes" of the Bible.

We are never given her name…perhaps because God would have us focus on her purpose? What was her purpose?

Here was a woman who had been plagued with an issue of blood (stayed on her cycle) for twelve years. Women will know that this was definitely an unsettled matter that required immediate attention!

The woman had tried everything to get well. The Bible tells us that she used all of her money hoping to find a cure…but she did not find healing in the many physicians that she consulted. Eventually, she sought out Jesus.

Our sister broke some rules.

- Her deliverance was more important than the opinion of the people.
- She did it without waiting for others to help her.
- She pressed her way through the crowd because her deliverance was too important to let Him pass her by.

Today, press your way past the issues and work your purpose. Your point and place of purpose are where you are, and what you can do to make things better around you. Please seek the face of God and the mind of Christ for today. Go hard after righteousness so that your purpose will be revealed to you; in doing so, you will find that you don't need to look to others for approval. God will fill you according to His promise.

> *"God blesses those who hunger and thirst for justice,*
> *for they will be satisfied."*
> ***Matthew 5:6 (NIV)***

Make it a great day!

What Do I Need to "Press Past" Today?

○— So, You Decided to Stay! —○

"Judge not, that ye be not judged."
Matthew 7:1 (KJV)

A heart can be broken, but it keeps beating just the same.

Let's say that you gave your heart to someone or something, and you didn't get back the same love that you put in. Maybe you were in a situation where the one you loved was loving someone else.

But you decided to stay...

- You stayed with that ministry.
- You stayed with that job.
- You stayed in that relationship.

If that was your choice, the formula to make it successful is simple.

- Acknowledge the betrayal. You were betrayed, and it hurt. Acknowledgment takes away the sting.
- Forgive the betrayal. Remember—forgiveness is about freeing *you!*
- Do not "rehearse" the betrayal. Don't warehouse it and keep pulling it out to go over and over it.

You decided to stay, and that means that you have given up your right to judge. *"Judge not so you won't be judged."* You didn't run out on your relationship...but you have your own faults.

Make it a great day!

Is There a Betrayal that I Need to Overcome Today?

Acknowledge...Forgive...Don't judge!

I Am a Designer Original

"I will praise thee, for I am fearfully and wonderfully made!"
Psalm 139:14 (KJV)

"The Color Purple" is my all-time favorite movie. I love the sister connection that Celie and Nettie had, and I love how Celie evolved from a caterpillar into a butterfly.

Celie didn't feel like she was a nobody. The men in her life made her feel that way. She was abused—sexually, mentally, verbally, and physically. She didn't feel like she was a nobody…but she *did* feel unloved.

Have you ever had a Celie moment? Maybe you are comparing yourself to others; the person who has a bigger house, when yours is hardly large enough for your family, or the person who has multiple degrees, while you barely made it out of high school.

Whatever and whoever you are, be the best you that you can be. *Be. Yourself.* God made you to show you to the world! How can you be your best self?

- **Tell** yourself: *"I am fearfully and wonderfully made!"*
- **Convince** yourself: *"God's works are wonderful!"*
- **Have confidence** in yourself: *"I know that full well."*

At the end, although her husband had tried over and over to beat her down, Celie was able to free herself. As she rode away, she said, *"I may be Black. I may be poor! I may even be ugly! But I'm still here!"* Say these words until you believe them. *"I am God's original masterpiece; there is no one like me…and I'm still here!"*

Make it a great day!

---

2 Spielberg, Steven, 1985. *The Color Purple*. United States: Warner Bros.

Is There an Area Where I Need to Work the Converse...Convince...Confidence Plan?

○— **Random Acts of Kindness** —○

*"Dear children, let us not love with words or speech but
with actions and in truth."*
1 John 3:18 (NIV)

Growing up at the King of Glory Tabernacle Church of God in Christ, our pastors' anniversary month was in May. Months before the anniversary, the announcer would say, *"It's time to put love in action."*

Putting Love in Action became the theme for Bishop Shephard Little and his lovely wife, Mother Elnora Little.

I learned that love is more than just a word…it is an action. God proved this to us in His Word when He said, *"For God so loved the world that He **gave** His only begotten Son…" **(John 3:16a, KJV)**. Love = Action!* I would even say that you cannot truly love without action. God loved us, and so we ought to love others.

Today, I challenge you to show love through a random act of kindness, honoring God by showing love to others. Some things you could do…

- Pay for the person in line behind you at the coffee shop.
- Send a *"Thinking about you…"* card to someone.
- Send a note to someone who is incarcerated.
- Text someone that you haven't talked to in a while and just say, *"Hey! I love you!"*

You are doing this from your heart, not to get something in return…but when you give, you often receive unexpectedly! My grandmother always said, *"It's nice to be nice."*

Make it a great day!

My Random Acts of Kindness for Today

○— Sing a Song —○

Singing brings *joy*—**Psalm 132:9**
Sing in *times of trouble*—**Acts 16:25**
The slaves sang for *freedom*—**Psalm 68:6**
Singing brings *strength*—**Psalm 81:1-2**
Singing is a form of *praise*—**Psalm 98:1**

Singing is more than just a "good sound." (And not all of us sound good when we sing!)

Singing is to our soul what oxygen is to our physical body. It has a way of reaching into the deepest parts of our soul and is an expression of love and response to God and His creation.

Choose a song, and let it create an atmosphere of praise, freedom, joy, and strength. One of my favorite songs is, *"His Eye is on the Sparrow."*

"I sing because I'm happy...I sing because I'm free! His eye is on the sparrow, and I know He watches me!"

The *assurance* is that He is watching over me. The *praise* is that He is watching over me. The *freedom* is that He is watching over me. The *joy* is that *He is watching over me!*

Sing, sing, sing! It will make you happy!

Make it a great day!

---

3 Civilla D. Martin and Charles H. Gabriel; *His Eye is On the Sparrow*, 1905,.

My Favorite Song

◦— Be Generous —◦

*"A generous person will prosper;
whoever refreshes others will be refreshed."*
Proverbs 11:25 (NIV)

"There is not a nation on the earth guilty of practices more shocking and bloody than are the people of the United States, at this very hour."

Frederick Douglas spoke these words in 1852, as a part of a speech entitled: *"What to the Slave is the Fourth of July?"* The United States was on the brink of the Civil War, and slavery was at the center of the conflict.

Here we are in the year 2020, almost 170 years later…and we have not made much progress. This year has exposed the "true character" of our hearts. Covid-19 has crippled the entire world. Our country is facing the injustices committed at the hands of those sworn to protect us. Systemic racism is still an issue, all these years later. *Black Lives Matter!* has become a rallying cry for those seeking change.

You can change the story. You can start by being generous. You need to be generous with your *time,* your *talents,* and your *love*.

- Be generous with your *time*. Make time in your schedule to help someone. Volunteer. Read to the elderly. Run errands for someone who is housebound.
- Be generous with your *talent*. God has gifted you with talents…are you *burying them* or *sharing them?*
- Be generous with your *love*. Love the unlovable, just as Christ has loved you in your own unlovable state.

Give of yourself generously, without expectations. If you want the world to be a better place to live in, start by being *generous*.

Make it a great day!

How Can I be Generous with My Time, Talent, or Love Today?

○— The Benefits of Waiting on God —○

*"But they that wait upon the Lord
shall renew their strength;
they shall mount up with wings as eagles;
they shall run, and not be weary;
and they shall walk, and not faint."*
Isaiah 40:31 (KJV)

"I know that God is going to make everything alright."

Speak those words into the atmosphere—it's going to be alright!

My problem is not whether or not I am *going* to win…I just want to know *when!*

Most of us want the manifestation of His promises quickly. Have you ever prayed *"Right now, God!"*? The reality is that we can count on one hand the number of times that we have seen the manifestation "right now."

God's timing is not our timing. But there *are* benefits to waiting on God.

- Your strength is renewed. He is giving you the strength that you need to endure while you wait.
- You will *"mount up and soar like eagles,"* meaning that you will exceed expectations!
- In the race you are running, you will not grow weary—and in this walk of faith, you will not faint.

God *will* deliver. Stand still, and see the salvation of the Lord!

Make it a great day!

What Manifestation am I Waiting on God for in My Life?

⊶ The Power of Prayer ⊷

*"And he spake a parable unto them to this end,
that men ought always to pray, and not to faint..."*
Luke 18:1 KJV

Two things to keep in mind today:

- Prayer is the *believer's lifeline*.
- The strategy of the enemy can be *overthrown* with prayer.

The Lifeline...

We have all heard someone say, *"Stay prayerful!"*, *"I am praying for you!"*, or *"Did you pray about it?"*

Why are we always pointed back to prayer? Because prayer is the *believer's lifeline!* Prayer is our connection, and our opportunity to spend time with God.

Just as our physical bodies need oxygen, our spiritual bodies need prayer. You need to pray to maintain your connection to God!

Have you ever been working on your computer and had the message, *"Internet connection is unstable."* flash across the screen? Our computers need the internet to function... just as we need God!

We cannot afford to have an unstable connection with God in this unstable environment that we are living in. *Prayer is our lifeline.*

The Power

Do you remember when Elisha was on Mount Carmel, fighting against the followers of Baal? They challenged him and said, *"The god that answers by fire, we shall serve."* Elisha prayed…and fire fell from heaven! The strategy of the enemy was overthrown!

I cannot tell you the number of times that I have received an unction from God telling me to look in my sons' room, or go to the school and see what my girls are up to, only to learn that they were getting into something that could have led to trouble.

"The prayers of the righteous availeth much…"

Simply put, this means that much is available to those who pray!

Today, be prayerful. It's your lifeline; and with your prayers, you are overthrowing the schemes of the enemy.

Make it a great day!

"I urge, then, first of all, that petitions, prayers, intercession and thanksgiving be made for all people."
1 Timothy 2:1 (NIV)

Prayer of **supplication**: Making your request known to God.

....

....

....

....

....

....

Prayer of **thanksgiving**: Thank Him for what He's done.

....

....

....

....

Prayer of **intercession**: Approach the throne for someone else.

....

....

....

....

....

○— Save the Babies —○

*"And all thy children shall be taught of the Lord;
and great shall be the peace of thy children."*
Isaiah 54:13 (KJV)

Linda Creed was diagnosed with breast cancer at the age of twenty-six. Despite the challenges that she faced, she continued to work, eventually teaming up with composer Michael Masser and writing the lyrics to *"The Greatest Love of All,"* which was the theme song for Muhammed Ali's biopic, simply titled *"The Greatest."* It would go on to be a hit for singer Whitney Houston in 1986.

Linda's purpose was to leave a legacy to the children, helping them find strength in the midst of their challenges, and giving them the confidence to push through and become successful, in spite of the odds that they may have faced.

Today, we declare the Word of God over our youth. We pray that they will be strong, successful overcomers. Let us band together, declaring that our children will be taught of the Lord—not just what we *tell* them but what we *show* them.

Let us show them that Jesus is the way, and declare over them that they will be a generation of seekers according to **Psalm 24:6**, which says, *"This is the generation of them that seek him, that seek thy face, O Jacob. Selah."*

Great peace shall be the future of our youth—in their minds, in their money, and in their ministry.

*"I believe the children are our future
Teach them well and let them lead the way
Show them all the beauty they possess inside
Give them a sense of pride to make it easier
Let the children's laughter remind us how we used to be..."*

Make it a great day!

A Prayer for My Children and Grandchildren

My personal prayer is for my grands—Taylor Shonnell, David III, Daniel Joel, Dayna Laniece, Dylan Elisha, London Taylor, Jamarya Renee, Dior Channel, Christin Leslie, Tyler Marcy, and Bonus!

○— Own Your Day! —○

*"This is the very day God acted—
let's celebrate and be festive!"*
Psalm 118:24c (MSG)

I declare today to be a ***No Foolishness Day!*** I own my day!

My goals are set. The things that I plan to accomplish include spending time with God in prayer, worship, reading His Word, and looking for opportunities to share Jesus.

- I will focus on moving *forward*, not *backward*.
- I will cleave to those things which are *good*.
- I will be an influencer through my *words* and *actions*.

Notice what is missing?

- Negative and unhealthy conversation.
- Toxicity and division.
- Unnecessary, unkind words and actions.
- Pity…and pettiness.

This is the day that the Lord has made; and to honor Him, we will rejoice and be glad in it!

Make it a great day!

Rejoice, Be Glad, No Foolishness; I Will Own My Day!

◦— Serve the Lord with Gladness! —◦

"A wife of noble character who can find?
She is worth far more than rubies.
Her husband has full confidence in her
and lacks nothing of value.
She brings him good, not harm,
all the days of her life."
Proverbs 31:10-12 (NIV)

My husband and I have been together since our senior year of high school. We are *that* couple who went to each other's prom and graduation! One of the greatest joys that I have is seeing something that I have done put a smile on his face. When he says after a meal, *"That was good eating,"* I smile because he liked what I made. Even after all these years, knowing that he likes something that I did or made brings me great joy.

I minister to him through cooking and making his house a place of peace. I don't do this because I think that he would "throw me away" if I didn't. I do it because of the love that I have for him.

The same can be said of our service to God. Why are you serving Him? Why are you a Kingdom Builder? Why do you go to church? Are you only on the battlefield because you don't want to go to hell? Are you afraid that He will "strike you down" if you don't perform?

We should seek to please God *not* because we fear the consequences of not doing so, but because it is our joy to please the One we love.

Make it a great day!

How Can I Serve the Lord Today with a Purpose, on Purpose?

Muzzle Your Mouth

*"Let the words of my mouth,
and the meditation of my heart,
be acceptable in thy sight, O Lord,
my strength, and my redeemer."*
Psalm 19:14 (KJV)

In this season we are in, everyone is wearing masks to keep the virus from entering our bodies. But how do we keep the "virus" out of our speech? How do keep our tongue from infecting those around us with our harsh words?

The tongue is a very powerful tool because it holds the power of life and death in its words.

Let the words of my mouth...
- Help me, Lord, to control my conversation. Is it true? Is it kind? Is it necessary?

And the meditation of my heart...
- I may be angry, but I will not allow my anger to dictate my outward expression. I will control my emotions.

Be acceptable in Thy sight...
- When my ways please the Lord, even my enemies will be at peace with me.

How will I accomplish all of this today? I will lean on God for He is my strength and my Redeemer. He gives me the ability to get things done. My strength comes from His power, which lives inside of me. And my Redeemer has delivered me from that which held me in bondage.

Make it a great day!

How Can I Ensure That my Words are Fruitful, Powerful, and Positive Today?

I Will...I Shall...
I *Must* Overcome!

"No, in all these things we are more than conquerors through him who loved us."
Romans 8:37 (NIV)

When I was in elementary school, we took spelling tests on Friday morning. To prepare for the test, we worked in our spellers every day. On Mondays, we would receive the words for that week, and our homework assignments included defining each word, writing it five times, matching it with the correct definition, and using it in a sentence. On Friday, the teacher would give us a sheet of paper and then have us write each word correctly. The lessons from the week were to prepare us for the test.

When it comes to spiritual matters, the process is reversed. We have to pass the test to learn the lesson. If you find yourself dealing with the same trial time and again, it's possible that you haven't learned the lesson!

Jesus walked through three years of public ministry with His disciples, and there were many tests along the way. I think that these tests were lessons, preparing them for the day when He was not there with them any longer, so that they could be overcomers.

The next time you find yourself in a test, search diligently for the lesson.

"I have told you these things, so that in me you may have peace. In this world you will have trouble. But take heart! I have overcome the world."
John 16:33 (NIV)

Make this your declaration as you go through today...

I will...I shall...I *must* overcome!

Make it a great day!

I Am an Overcomer

Have Your Way, Lord!

*"I will consider all your works
and meditate on all your mighty deeds."
Your ways, God, are holy.
What god is as great as our God?"*
Psalm 77:12-13 (NIV)

The Psalmist is showing us God's movement through His work, through His will, and through His Word.

God is moving through His work.
Who is so great as our God? Who can do the things He does? When we meditate on the work of God, not only does it give us some relief from our present circumstances, but it serves as a reminder that *if He did it before, He can do it again!*

God is moving through His will.
"Thy way" is how one version describes His will. Why has God not stopped all of the calamity in your life? Because He is moving in His will, and His will is holy.

God is moving through His Word.
Speaking of what He is doing in our lives to others builds our faith and draws others to Him.

When we ask God to "have His way," we are really saying, *"Move, God. Move through Your will, Your way, and Your work."*

When the Word of God connects with the Spirit of God, expect the amazing! *Have your way, Lord!*

Make it a great day!

Word of God + Spirit of God = the Amazing! Put the Word on It!

○— The Heart of the Matter! —○

*"Keep thy heart with all diligence;
for out of it are the issues of life."*
Proverbs 4:23 (KJV)

Your heart is very important to your mental and spiritual health. It houses your emotions and displays your character.

The warrior David had to go before the Lord after his affair with Bathsheba. He asked the Lord to create in him a "clean heart," for he knew that if his heart was clean, his flesh would follow.

As you go forward today, watch what goes into your heart. Do not allow the hurt and pain of your environment to penetrate your heart and take up residence. This does not mean you won't get hurt, but do not let it take up permanent space in your heart. Release the pain, and replace it with things that make you smile. Find your happy place.

Watch what comes out of your heart. The Scriptures tell us that *"from the heart flow the issues of life."* If bitterness is in your heart, your speech will be bitter. If your heart is kind, then you will speak kindly. Watch what comes out because we want to represent the Lord well in our lives.

Watch what covers your heart. If your heart is covered correctly, you will be able to discern that which is good and that which is evil. Cover your heart with the Word of God.

Make it a great day!

What Is Covering My Heart Today?

○— Help Me to Handle this Moment —○

"...weeping may endure for a night..."
Psalm 30:5d (KJV)

I went to bed one night with a heavy heart. The things happening in the world—the pandemic, systematic racism, the unrest of our young people, and the spiritual wickedness in high places, coupled with personal battles—caused me to be in a place where only I could pull myself out from.

How did I get here? How did I let someone's opinion destroy my joy? I thought what I did was right. My intentions were good; and yet, I ended up here? When did the hate start, and why is it so intense that legal action against me is a possibility?

My hurt feelings wanted to tell anyone who would listen just why I was in this place. The Holy Spirit, who is my Sustainer and my Keeper, coached me to take a different approach. I gotta go greater!

The first thing that I realized was that I missed the signs that things were not as they were supposed to be.

The second lesson was more painful. I learned that not everyone can handle my hurt places. I thank God for my husband, who is able to be there in those places with me.

Finally, I realized that this was a momentary experience. I prayed to my dear God and asked Him to help me. My utmost desire is to please Him.

*"God is our refuge and strength,
an ever-present help in trouble."*
Psalm 46:1 (NIV)

He is not only *present* in this moment...He is *my present* to handle this moment.

> *"God is in the midst of her; she shall not be moved:*
> *God shall help her, and that right early."*
> ***Psalm 46:5 (KJV)***

After a while, this will all be over. The mindset must be that we will not return to normal, but *greater*…GFG!

Make it a great day!

My Name is _____, and I am Going for Greater Today By…

You Have What You Need for a
○— Great Day! —○

"Trust in the Lord with all thine heart; and lean not unto thine own understanding. In all thy ways acknowledge him, and he shall direct thy paths."
Proverbs 3:5-6 (KJV)

I was in the car traveling from one part of Chicago to another. Not quite familiar with my destination, I pushed the button in the car that has all the answers. The voice asked me where I wanted to go and I gave it the address. The directions were then downloaded to my vehicle.

I trusted that voice because I paid for it to tell me how to get where I need to go, and I followed the directions until I got to my destination…and drove right past it! I heard the voice say, *"You have left the planned route."*

God is that voice for us. We have put our trust in God to lead and guide us…yet, there are times when we are guided by what is in front of us, and "leave the route."

Acknowledge that God knows everything, from the beginning of your day to the end…and *don't leave the planned route.*

Make it a great day!

Have I "Left the Planned Route" in Any Area of My Life?

I Am

I am a *faith walker*…not a *fear dweller*.

I am free from the guilt of my past because *mercy has no memory* and *grace has no regrets*.

I am *above* and not *beneath*—I am not a doormat.

I am anointed *on* purpose, *for* a purpose. I am not available to house other's insecurities.

I walk in *victory*. I am not a victim of self-pity.

I am *peaceful*, and I *walk in peace* in my mind, body, ministry, finances, and family. I am not a conduit of confusion.

I am *more than a conqueror*. I am not defeated.

I have the Lord as my Light and my Salvation…and *I am not afraid*.

I have *everything that I need* for life and godliness…and I will not suffer lack.

I am a *promise*…I am *not* a mistake.

I am *everything* that God says I am!

Make it a great day!

My "I Am" Declaration

◦— Break the Rules —◦

*"For you were once darkness, but now you are
light in the Lord. Live as children of light."*
Ephesians 5:8 (NIV)

Lazarus was dead and had been in his tomb for four days. Jesus "broke the rules" of death and said, *"Lazarus, come forth."*

Jesus had a crowd that followed Him and they needed to be fed. The disciples brought Him two fish and five loaves of bread. Jesus "broke the rules" of catering and fed 5,000 men, not including women and children.

Moses and the children of Israel had the Red Sea in front of them, mountains on either side, and Pharaohs' army behind. God "broke the rules" of water and pulled back the sea, creating the world's first "superhighway" for the children of Israel to walk across to freedom.

Maybe the doctor tells you that this condition is going to last for the rest of your life. Jesus is "breaking the rules" of medicine.

There are things going on all around your world; but you have unspeakable joy. God is "breaking the rules" of confusion.

My family accuses me of occasionally breaking the rules when we are playing games…but I only break them to win! Jesus is breaking the rules so that *we* will win.

Single mothers, you *can* raise successful children.

Singles, you *can* be satisfied in your time of singleness.

"Minimum wage" does *not* mean "minimum living."

Your marriage *can* survive in this age of divorce.

God is still breaking the rules! Don't focus on what you *see*. Focus on what you *know!* Thanks be to God, who always causes us to triumph!

Make it a great day!

Where Do I Need to "Break the Rules" in My Life?

The Man in the Mirror

"For as a man thinketh in his heart, so is he."
Proverbs 23:7 (KJV)

Before leaving home, most of us take a look in the mirror to make sure that everything is in place and that our look "reflects us."

How you live your life is connected to "the man in the mirror," your true self. It is a reflection of what and who you are inside.

God has equipped you with the power to be an overcomer: great, powerful, and victorious.

If you are looking in the mirror and you don't see those qualities, you can change! What you think about yourself should reflect who God says you are.

- Your *praise* should reflect your *victory*.
- Your *giving* should reflect your *receiving*.
- Your *faith* should reflect your *breakthrough*.
- Your *walk* should reflect your *healing*.
- Your *behavior* should reflect your *character*.

Make it a great day!

What Does God Say About Me Today?

○— Live Your Best Life Today —○

"The thief cometh not, but for to steal, and to kill, and to destroy: I am come that they might have life, and that they might have it more abundantly."
John 10:10 (KJV)

Fish function better in water.
Airplanes function better in the air.
Cereal functions better in milk.
Trains function better on the tracks.
You function better when you live your best life as God intended.

Today, strive to live your best life possible because…

- It honors God. *"…present your bodies a living sacrifice, holy, acceptable unto God, which is your reasonable service…"* ***Romans 12:1 (KJV)***
- It will make you a better witness, and you will attract others to God.
- It makes you a better person.

Best life living is not contingent on the things that you possess materially but rather on what you possess *spiritually*.

Make it a great day!

How Am I Living My Best Life?

Heal and Restore

> *"For I will restore health unto thee,
> and I will heal thee of thy wounds."*
> ***Jeremiah 30:17a (KJV)***

2020 will go down in history as one of the worst years the world has ever seen, and I believe that we all share that sentiment.

We have been wounded by systemic racism which resulted in the injury or death of many African Americans. Sadly, many of those died at the hands of those who were sworn to "serve and protect," and some of those were not prosecuted to the fullest extent of the law. It has been a painful year that has left us deeply wounded as a people.

Shall we bring it closer to home? Have you experienced things that have left you broken? It is important that you don't put a Band-Aid on a wound that needs surgery.

God wants us to be healed and restored.

If you are to believe God for your healing, there are two things you must do:

- Stop watching the clock. Have you ever said, *"I thought I would be over this by now…"*? Time will help us to heal, but God's timing is different from ours. Trust and believe that He's on it!
- Change your narrative! Let your conversation be more about healing and restoration. *"Death and life are in the power of the tongue."* ***Proverbs 18:21 (KJV)***

Make it a great day!

What is the Lesson that God Wanted Me to Learn from 2020?

Dear God, Accomplish Your
○— Will in My Life —○

"Draw nigh to God, and he will draw nigh to you."
James 4:8 (KJV)

There are things that God wants to accomplish in us. I invite you to take a personal journey, creating time and space to hear from the Lord.

God responds when we make a diligent effort to get closer to Him.

Take the time to seek God for His will and for your purpose. The Syrophoenician woman is a good example of chasing after God and His will.

It started with a need. Her daughter had an unclean spirit, and she had faith that Jesus had the ability to heal. She sought Him out, worshipped Him, and stayed close to His Word. Jesus rewarded her faith by restoring her daughter.

Seek God. Worship Him, and stay close to His Word. He will accomplish His purpose in your life.

Make it a great day!

What Am I Seeking God for Today?

React or Respond

"Man that is born of a woman is of few days and full of trouble."
Job 14:1 (KJV)

We can expect tension in our lives. How should we react? How should we respond?

Reaction is laced with emotion and performance. Response, I would argue, is a reply that is given with thought.

For a perfect example of reaction vs. response, we only need to look at the life of Jesus.

There was a woman who was caught in the act of adultery, and the Pharisees were about to stone her. Jesus didn't react—He responded by writing in the sand and challenging anyone who was without sin to cast the first stone.

I love Jesus!

Go out into the world, and be who you were born to be—great. In every situation, be gentle (*response*), because harshness (*reaction*) causes anger.

"A gentle answer turns away wrath, but a harsh word stirs up anger."
Proverbs 15:1 (NIV)

Make it a great day!

When Life Comes at Me, How Do I React? How Do I Respond?

◦— Burned but Not Buried —◦

On January 4, 1971, my sister Romelle Diane Taylor came home after a freezing cold commute from downtown Chicago to our home in Park Manor.

Chicago winters are brutally cold, and Romelle wanted to get warm as quickly as possible, so she layered her body with her nylon nightgown, flannel pajamas, and a robe, then stood close to the stove where a pot was cooking on the burner.

Tragically, she stood too close to the stove; and before anyone could react, my sister was on fire. As my brother Jeffery and I watched in horror, our mother walked in the door, removed her coat, and smothered the fire that had engulfed my sister's back. (My mother, Bettye Taylor, has been smothering fires, both literally and figuratively, all of my life. Thank God for my mother!)

Romelle spent months at the University of Chicago Hospital. I still remember the smells—the smell of her skin as she was on fire and the smell of the salve that was used on her daily to help her heal. With the exception of a few scars, the salve worked, and Romelle was *burned*…but not *buried*.

We have all experienced many burns in life…but they don't have to bury who we are and what we want to accomplish.

> *"Is there no balm in Gilead?*
> *Is there no physician there?*
> *Why then is there no healing*
> *for the wound of my people?"*
> **Jeremiah 8:22 (NIV)**

Yes, there is a balm (salve) that we can use for our burns. His name is Jesus, and He has given us His Word to apply to every wound, every burn, and every pain that we have. Using it on the wound daily will usher in our healing. Don't worry about the scar that it may leave in your heart—it serves as a reminder that God brought you out once, and He will do it again!

Make it a great day!

Is There a Wound in My Life that ⊶ Needs Healing? ⊸

*"Heal me, Lord, and I will be healed;
save me and I will be saved,
for you are the one I praise."*
Jeremiah 17:14 (NIV)

About the Author

Elder Lisa T. Ballard is a proud member of the Sunrise Full Gospel Baptist Church of Chicago, Illinois, where her husband of forty-one years, Pastor David Ballard, Sr., serves as the senior pastor. Lisa and David heeded the call of God upon their lives, which brought them together in their love for Jesus, for their ministry, and for each other. Through passionate oratory, biblical teaching, and unwavering faith in the Gospel of Jesus Christ, this dynamic duo has turned Sunrise Church into a pillar of Chicago's Englewood community.

In December 2000, Lisa was ordained as an elder, becoming the first pastors' wife in the history of Sunrise Church to obtain this high honor. She is a mentor, motivator, and inspiration to many.

As co-founder and leader of the Sistah-2-Sistah Ministry, she displays her heart through her wisdom and her personal testimony as a minister, wife, mother, and grandmother—a living example of the **Proverbs 31** woman. Lisa has embraced Jesus' command to *"Go into all the world, and preach the good news to all creation."* Her preaching is filled with humor, transparency, and humility, captivating audiences and crossing the barriers of denomination, race, and age. She has carried this ministry from church to church, as well as into prisons, schools, and conferences across the United States.

Lisa considers raising a multitalented family to be her greatest achievement, and she takes great pride in seeing them minister both in and out of the pulpit.

- David II and Donishisa (Pastors – Word Worship Center of Rockford, IL)
- Denesha Trinnette
- D'Lisa and Jermel Flannigan (Pastor – Jerusalem Missionary Baptist Church of Rockford, IL)
- Renee Marie

What gives Lisa Ballard the biggest smile? Her ten grandchildren!

Taylor, David III, Daniel, Dayna, Dylan, London, Jamarya, Dior, Christin, Tyler…and bonus grand, Tenia Woods.

"If anyone should ever write my life story, please make sure they tell the world that Jesus is the best thing that ever happened to me!"

Contact the Author

Email
lballardministries@gmail.com

Facebook
Elder Lisa Ballard - Ballard Ministries

Instagram
Lisa T. Ballard

Twitter
@ltballard

www.ingramcontent.com/pod-product-compliance
Lightning Source LLC
Chambersburg PA
CBHW051406290426
44108CB00015B/2175